Reel It In
FLY-FISHING

Tina P. Schwartz

PowerKiDS
press™

New York

To Heather… 'Cause you're so fly! — with love, Mom

Published in 2012 by The Rosen Publishing Group, Inc.
29 East 21st Street, New York, NY 10010

First Edition

Editor: Amelie von Zumbusch
Book Design: Kate Laczynski

Photo Credits: Cover, p. 13 (top) H. Mark Weidman/Getty Images; pp. 4–5 Karl Weatherly/Digital Vision/Thinkstock; p. 6 David Deas/Getty Images; pp. 7, 20 Jupiterimages/Liquidlibrary/Thinkstock; pp. 8, 9 iStockphoto/Thinkstock; pp. 10–11 Photodisc/Thinkstock; pp. 12, 17 (top), 19 (top) Shutterstock.com; p. 13 (bottom) Patrice Hauser/Getty Images; p. 14 © www.iStockphoto.com/Sean Boggs; p. 15 Don Mason/Getty Images; p. 16 Earl Harper/Getty Images; p. 17 (bottom) © www.iStockphoto.com/Robert Dant; p. 18 © www.iStockphoto.com/Joe Michl; p. 19 (bottom) © www.iStockphoto.com/Kevin Miller; p. 21 © Steve Smith/Purestock/SuperStock; p. 22 © www.iStockphoto.com/Karen Massier.

Library of Congress Cataloging-in-Publication Data

Schwartz, Tina P., 1969–
 Fly-fishing / by Tina P. Schwartz. — 1st ed.
     p. cm. — (Reel it in)
 Includes index.
 ISBN 978-1-4488-6198-9 (library binding) — ISBN 978-1-4488-6355-6 (pbk.) — ISBN 978-1-4488-6356-3 (6-pack)
 1. Fly fishing—Juvenile literature. I. Title.
 SH456.S3629 2012
 799.12'4—dc23
                              2011027916

Manufactured in the United States of America

CPSIA Compliance Information: Batch #WW12PK: For Further Information contact Rosen Publishing, New York, New York at 1-800-237-9932

CONTENTS

What Is Fly-Fishing?

Fly-fishing is one of the hardest ways to fish. This is because it depends on a special method of **casting** your line. It is different from other types of casting.

When you fly-fish, you use a fly at the end of your line. A fly is a hook with feathers or other things tied around it. Flies are made to look like insects or other things that fish eat. When you cast your line, your fly should land on top of the water or just below it. If you make the fly move like a real insect, you can trick a fish into trying to eat it!

FUN FISH FACT

When a fish takes your fly, it is called a strike. The movement a person makes in order to hook a fish is also known as a strike.

The lines used in fly-fishing are quite long. Casting requires a wide-open space. You do not want your line to get tangled up in trees, wires, or bushes.

Fly-Fishing Gear

This boy is wearing a fishing vest. Fishing vests have lots of pockets. These are good for holding flies and other things.

To go fly-fishing, you need a rod and **reel**, or spool of line. You will also need a **leader** and **tippet**. These connect the fly to the fishing line. In most places, you will need to get a fishing **license**, too.

Many fly fishermen **wade**, or walk, into the water to fish. People who do this often wear waterproof pants, called **waders**. These keep a fisherman, or **angler**, warm and dry. Smart anglers also bring along sunglasses, hats, and rain gear. That way they will be ready for any kind of weather.

The line used in fly-fishing is often known as fly line. Fly line comes in different weights. Each fly-fishing pole is made to work with fly line of a certain weight.

Different Types of Flies

There are thousands of kinds of flies you can use when fly-fishing. Two of the main types are dry flies and wet flies. Wet flies float below the surface of the water. Many look like insects that fell into the water and could be food.

Fly-fishing flies are made out of many things, such as feathers, animal hair, and thread. Flies are also sometimes called lures.

This fly fisherman is picking which fly to use. If you are having trouble picking a fly, look at the insects near the water. Then pick a fly that looks a bit like these insects.

Dry flies rest on the surface of the water. Most look like insects that rest on the water's surface. Dry flies that are made to draw larger fish may look like bigger animals, such as frogs. One fun thing about using dry flies is that you can see the fish jump out of the water to strike!

How to Cast Your Line

When you cast, you should hold your rod like you would hold someone's hand while shaking hands. Your thumb should point toward the rod's tip. There are four main ways to cast your line. These are the overhead cast, the backhand cast, the roll cast, and the side cast.

An overhead cast is the most basic cast. It has two parts. These are a back cast followed by a front cast. To back cast, pull your rod up. The line should fly up and then stretch out behind you in a straight line. Then snap the rod forward to front cast.

You should hold on to your rod firmly while casting. Do not hold it too tightly, though. This can make your hand tired.

FUN FISH FACT

Before you cast your line, have an adult help you get your gear ready. Put together the rod and reel. Put line through the rod. Tie on the leader, tippet, and fly.

Fishing in Different Waters

Common places to go fly-fishing are in ponds, lakes, small streams, larger rivers, and even the ocean. Fishing in clear, cold water will bring you the best results when fishing for trout, salmon, and steelheads.

Fish that live in rivers and streams usually let the flow of water bring them food while they stay in one place. That is why many fly fishermen wade into the water to fish.

Fish are good at sensing sounds and movements in the water. This means you need to walk slowly and carefully when wading in a creek such as this one.

Some fly fishermen cast their lines from boats. This lets you fish in areas that are too deep to wade in.

Learning to cast quickly is key for saltwater fly-fishing. Fish in the ocean tend to move around more than fish in freshwater do.

Fish would love to find a safe place to hide from you. They often hide in shadowy areas or under trees or rocks. Fish hide by going very deep into the water, too.

Nice Catch!

The person who caught this rainbow trout is releasing it.

After you catch a fish, you can let it go back into the wild. This is known as **catch-and-release** fishing. Before you let your fish go, have an adult help you remove the hook. Then put the fish in water. Softly move the fish back and forth to get water moving through its **gills**. Gills are what fish use to breathe.

You can also eat the fish you catch. If you decide to do this, ask an adult to help you clean and prepare the fish. Some people like to keep their catch as a **trophy**, or prize. They stuff and mount the fish. This makes a wonderful memory for any angler.

If you want to remember your catch but plan to release it, you can ask someone to take a picture of you with the fish before you let it swim away.

Many Kinds of Fish

Fly fishermen catch many kinds of fish. You can catch pike, crappies, bluegills, smallmouth bass, and largemouth bass in rivers and lakes. If you go fly-fishing in the ocean, you can catch saltwater fish. These include bluefish, shad, tuna, mackerel, and barracuda.

In the northeastern United States, anglers often look for **landlocked** Atlantic salmon. These fish live in bodies of water surrounded by land, such as

This man caught a tarpon while fishing off the island of Great Inagua, in the Bahamas. These saltwater fish are most often found in waters not too far off the coast.

Largemouth bass often jump out of the water and throw themselves around after they have been caught. This makes it fun to catch one when you are fly-fishing.

lakes. Other Atlantic salmon spend part of their lives in the ocean. Anglers catch these salmon along the coast or when they swim up rivers to lay eggs. Anglers catch several kinds of Pacific salmon in western rivers and the Pacific Ocean.

This boy caught a bluegill. Bluegills are also known as bream, brim, perch, sunfish, and sun perch.

Catching Trout

This is a rainbow trout. Some rainbow trout live their whole lives in freshwater. Rainbow trout that spend part of their lives in the ocean are called steelheads.

Trout are the fish that fly fishermen most often try to catch. There are several kinds of trout. Gila trout and Apache trout live in the American Southwest. People brought brown trout from Europe to North America because they liked fishing for them so much!

Rainbow trout are a favorite fish for many anglers. Fast-flowing streams are great places

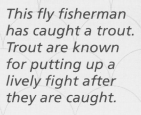

This fly fisherman has caught a trout. Trout are known for putting up a lively fight after they are caught.

to catch these fish. They are less bothered by light than other trout. They feed at the water's surface even on sunny days.

It is hard to catch trout in big lakes. They hide deep in the lakes. Pay attention to the edges of deep lakes, though. Some trout feed along the shore.

This boy caught a trout while fly-fishing in a lake.

19

The Fly-Fishing Community

Fly-fishing can be hard. Luckily, there are lots of people in the fly-fishing community who are happy to teach others their skills. Some people offer tips on casting. Others can tell you where to look for fish. Still others can show you how to make your own flies.

If you know someone who is good at fly-fishing, you can ask that person to show you how to cast your line.

People can teach you about fly-fishing's long, rich history, too. No one is exactly sure how the sport started. The Roman author Aelian was one of the first people to write about it, though. In AD 200, he wrote about fishermen in Macedonia who tied feathers and red wool around a hook and used it to catch fish!

Making flies is sometimes known as fly tying. The thing that is holding the fly that this man is making is a fly-tying vise.

Fly-Fishing in the Years to Come

Some places where fish live have become so polluted that the fish cannot survive there. Almost 80 **species**, or kinds, of fish are in danger of dying out in US waters. Trout are no longer found in about 85 percent of waters in which they once lived.

People are working to make the waters better for fish,

Wild places often are the best spots for fly-fishing. Anglers are working to make sure the best fly-fishing spots stay in their wild state.

though. Some fly fishermen use catch-and-release fishing. This keeps species from getting **overfished**. Others in the fly-fishing community work to keep lakes, streams, rivers, and oceans clean.

GLOSSARY

angler (ANG-gler) A person who fishes with a rod and reel.

casting (KAS-ting) Throwing a fishing line with a rod.

catch-and-release (kach-und-rih-LEES) A fishing method in which people let the fish they catch go.

gills (GILZ) Body parts that fish use for breathing.

landlocked (LAND-lokt) Not bordering or flowing into an ocean.

leader (LEE-der) The fine line that joins the fly to the fishing line.

license (LY-suns) Official permission to do something.

overfished (oh-ver-FISHD) Being caught in numbers that are too big.

reel (REEL) Something around which line or thread is wound.

species (SPEE-sheez) One kind of living thing. All people are one species.

tippet (TIH-pet) The thin end of a leader, which is a line that ties a fishing fly to fishing line.

trophy (TROH-fee) An exact copy of a fish made to show others one's catch.

wade (WAYD) To walk through water.

waders (WAY-derz) Pants or overalls worn to walk through water.

INDEX

WEB SITES

Due to the changing nature of Internet links, PowerKids Press has developed an online list of Web sites related to the subject of this book. This site is updated regularly. Please use this link to access the list: www.powerkidslinks.com/reel/fly/